Do You Wanna Bet?

Do You Wanna Bet?

Your Chance to Find Out About Probability

by JEAN CUSHMAN

Illustrated by MARTHA WESTON

CLARION BOOKS • NEW YORK

My thanks to Irma Schwartz, for useful materials, and to my writers' group colleagues for advice and encouragement. Their help greatly increased the probability that this book would be written.

The idea for the probability worksheet on page 18 was suggested by an exercise in *What Are My Chances?* (Book A) by Albert P. Shulte and Stuart A. Choate (Palo Alto, Calif.: Creative Publications, Inc., 1977).

Clarion Books
a Houghton Mifflin Company imprint
215 Park Avenue South, New York, NY 10003
Text copyright © 1991 by Jean Cushman
Illustrations copyright © 1991 by Martha Weston
First Clarion paperback edition, 2007.

The illustrations were executed in pencil.

www.clarionbooks.com

Printed in the U.S.A.

The Library of Congress has cataloged the hardcover edition as follows:

Cushman, Jean.
Do you wanna bet? : your chance to find out about probability / by Jean Cushman ; illustrated by Martha Weston.
p. cm.
Summary: Two boys find that the most ordinary events and activities such as card games, coin flips, sports scores and statistics, and even weather prediction are dependent on the subtle interplay of many factors of chance and probability.
Includes bibliographical references and index.
ISBN 0-395-56516-2
1. Probabilities—Juvenile literature. [1. Probabilities.] I. Weston, Martha, ill. II. Title.
QA273.16.C87   1991
519.2—dc20   90-44198
CIP   AC

CL ISBN-13: 978-0-395-56516-2   CL ISBN-10: 0-395-56516-2
PA ISBN-13: 978-0-618-82999-6   PA ISBN-10: 0-618-82999-7

EB 10
4500554922

For Mary, Bob, and Martha Cushman.

Contents

Do You Wanna Bet?

Do You Wanna Bet?

How lucky are you?

Are you a winner or a loser?

Probably sometimes you win. Other times you lose. You can't tell what the outcome will be when you:

- toss a coin;
- roll a die;
- spin a spinner;
- pick up a hand in a game of cards;
- plan an activity that requires good weather.

Your chances for success depend on *probability*. If you know more about probability, you are more likely to be a winner.

Turn the page to meet Brian and Danny. Are they winners or losers? Take your chances with them as they explore probability. You may be smarter than they are.

Do you wanna bet?

One Out of Two

Heads or Tails?

Danny Johnson wanted to watch *Ace Detective*. His friend Brian O'Shea wanted the ball game. They decided to flip a coin to choose which show to see.

Danny handed Brian a quarter. "Heads or tails?" he asked.

"Tails," answered Brian. He tossed the quarter. It landed heads up.

"That's it. We watch *Ace Detective*," Danny said.

"Nah. That's a stupid show," Brian objected. "I want to see what my team's doing. Let's flip again."

"OK," Danny agreed. "Make it two out of three. Heads or tails?"

"Tails."

Danny tossed. Heads again. He tuned the television set to *Ace Detective*.

"No way." Brian wasn't giving up. "*You* tossed the coin. Let's make it three out of five."

"Heads or tails?" asked Danny.

"I still say tails," answered Brian. He flipped the coin. Heads. That was the third toss, but Brian didn't stop. He tried throwing it over his shoulder. Heads. He spit on the coin, rubbed it, talked to it. "Nice coin, pretty coin, good coin, turn tails for me." He tossed again. Heads.

"Dumb coin. What do you know? Nothing! You're supposed to turn tails." Brian was angry. "What's with this quarter? Where'd you get it? I bet it's fixed some-how, so it always lands heads up."

"Wanna bet?"

"Yeah, I'll bet."

"How much?"

"A candy bar."

"OK." Brian rubbed the coin in his palm, kissed it, spoke softly. "Come on baby, once more baby, land heads up."

Do You Wanna Bet?

What are Brian's chances of winning the toss? Despite the long run of heads, will the coin land heads up once more?

• • •

☞ To find out the answers to these questions, keep reading.

Brian's Chances: Heads or Tails

Brian may win, or he may lose. Brian and Danny tossed Danny's quarter six times in a row. The first five times it came down heads. On each separate toss, the coin could have landed heads up *or* tails up. There were two possibilities, so the probability of heads was one out of two (1/2). What happened on one toss had no effect on what happened on the next. The probability of its coming down heads six times in a row was $1/2 \times 1/2 \times 1/2 \times 1/2 \times 1/2 \times 1/2$, or 1/64. But Brian was betting on only the *last* toss, so his chances were still one out of two. He still needed to be lucky in order to win. He wasn't. The coin landed tails up. He owed Danny a candy bar.

Brian is right about one thing. A coin is dumb. It doesn't know it has landed heads up three or four times in a row and that, to be fair, it should land tails up the next. Who tosses it or how it's tossed—overhand, underhand, for a short or long distance—makes no difference. The boys tossed the quarter six times. The first five times it landed heads up. On the sixth toss it landed tails up. If they had tossed it one hundred times, the totals for heads and for tails probably would have come close to fifty each—forty-six and fifty-four, for example. The more often a coin is tossed, the closer the number of heads and the number of tails will come to being equal.

Now You Try It: Coin Toss

1 ★ Toss a coin many times. You can do it by yourself, but it will be more fun if you do it with a friend. Keep track of your tosses with H for heads and T for tails, like this: HHTHHHTTHTTHHTH . . . Also use tally marks:

Heads: ⅠⅠⅠⅠ ⅠⅠⅠⅠ
Tails: ⅠⅠⅠⅠ Ⅰ

Which side of your coin was ahead after ten tosses? Twenty? Fifty? One hundred? Did the total number of heads come closer to being the same as the total of tails as you kept on tossing the coin? Did your coin ever land on heads or on tails five or more times in a row?

2 ★ Try tossing two different coins at the same time—a dime and a penny, for example. How many different combinations can you make? The dime and penny can both land heads up (HH). They can both land tails up (TT). The dime can land heads up while the penny lands tails up (HT), or the dime can land tails up with the penny heads up (TH). What are the chances that both coins will land heads up? There are four possible outcomes, so the chances are one out of four (1/4). You can also multiply the chances with the dime, one out of two, by the chances with the penny, one out of two (1/2 × 1/2), to get the same answer (1/4)—one chance out of four that both coins will land heads up. Using tally marks to keep track, toss your coins enough times to show that this is true.

Which Hand?

The boys settled down to watch *Ace Detective*. They didn't notice that Danny's little sister, Melissa, had wandered into the den until she reached for the remote control. "I want to watch *Sesame Street*," she said.

"Come on, Missy. You get to watch while we're in school. It's our turn now," said Danny.

"I want *Sesame*."

Danny grabbed his sister's favorite doll. He hid it behind his back. Baby Dear was out of sight.

"Which hand?" he asked.

Missy pointed to the right. Danny showed her an empty hand. She pointed to the left. Nothing.

"Show me! Show me both hands," she said.

"No. Choose one."

Missy pointed to the right. No doll. "Mommy! Mommy!" she cried. She ran toward the kitchen.

"Give her back her doll," Mrs. Johnson told the boys. "Come on now. You can help me bake cookies, Missy."

Danny rolled his eyes at Brian as he handed Missy her doll. Missy hugged Baby Dear. She followed her mother out to the kitchen.

When the boys finally turned back to the television, both *Ace Detective* and the baseball game were over.

"Let's go outside," Danny suggested. He picked up a ball and bat on the way out.

Do You Wanna Bet?

The next time Missy chooses which hand, will she get it right the first time? What are her chances?

Missy's Chances: Which Hand?

If Danny cheats again, Missy doesn't have a chance. If he plays fair, her chances are one out of two. The doll has to be in one hand or the other.

The chances are the same as those in a single coin toss. The coin has to land on one side or the other.

Girl or Boy?

Mrs. Johnson was the last to sit down at the dinner table. "Look," she said. She patted her round, high tummy. "The baby's so big, I can hardly reach over him."

"Him?" Danny's dad said. "You always say 'him.' Why are you so sure the baby is a boy?"

"I'm not, but I don't like to say 'it' all the time. That sounds like a doll, or an animal. This baby that's coming is a person, not a thing. A very important person."

"It's a boy. I know it. It's going to be a boy." Danny was sure. "I want a boy."

"How come?" Dad asked.

"You want another one like *her*?" He pointed at Missy. She stuck out her tongue.

"Sure. Why not? I'd like another little girl." Dad smiled at his daughter.

"I want a baby sister." Missy slipped out of her chair. She patted her mother's big belly. "Be a girl, little baby. Please."

"Boy, girl, I don't care. Just come soon, little-one-to-be. You're wearing me out." Mrs. Johnson sighed.

"Not much longer to wait. Danny, you clear the table. I'll serve dessert." Dad ended the discussion.

Do You Wanna Bet?

Will Danny get the baby brother he wants so much? What are his chances?

Danny's Chances: Girl or Boy?

Danny's chances of having a baby brother are close to Missy's of having a baby sister: about one out of two. But having a baby is different from tossing a coin. The results of a fair coin toss are determined by chance, or probability. Heredity and other factors may influence the sex of a baby.

Read to the end of the book to find out whether the Johnsons' new baby is a girl or a boy.

Forecasting

Will It Snow Tomorrow?

"It can't snow. It's the first day of spring!" Brian said to Danny.

"But it is snowing. Look out the window." Danny pointed.

"Yeah, maybe. Maybe it'll snow a lot. Then we won't have school tomorrow. A snow day in March! Let's not do our homework."

"We'd better check with the weather forecast," Danny suggested. He pressed the buttons on the telephone for the weather number.

A recorded voice answered: "Cloudy tonight. Winds ten to fifteen miles per hour from the northeast. Temperatures in the thirties. Sixty percent chance of snow this evening. Six to eight inches by morning."

"Hey, no school tomorrow, I bet. I'm not doing those math problems." Brian persuaded Danny to forget his homework, too. Both boys watched TV until Brian had to go home to dinner.

Do You Wanna Bet?

What were the chances that it would snow? Was it safe for Brian and Danny to skip their homework?

Brian and Danny's Chances:
Will It Snow Tomorrow?

This bet was too risky. The chances were sixty out of one hundred (60%) that there would be enough snow to close school. But there were still forty chances out of one hundred (40%) that school would be held. Forty percent is too close to even chances, fifty out of one hundred (50%), or fifty-fifty. Even if the forecaster had predicted a 100 percent chance of snow, the boys should have done their homework. The National Weather Service does not control the weather. It cannot be 100 percent correct.

How do forecasters make predictions? They observe what is happening outside and learn what is happening where the weather comes from. Then they compare their findings with what has happened under the same or similar conditions in the past. If snow fell under certain conditions sixty out of one hundred times in the past, they announce that there is a 60 percent chance of snow when those same conditions are repeated.

Brian can't control the weather any more than the forecaster can. He can wish for snow, but he can't make it. He couldn't control a coin either. Brian seems unlucky. Maybe he is just hoping for more luck than he can expect to have.

Now You Try It: Predicting the Weather

Keep track of the weather forecast and the actual weather for a number of days. If the forecaster says that the chances of rain or snow are 50 percent or higher, count that forecast as a prediction of rain or snow. For each day the prediction is correct, write the number 1. For each day it is not, write 0. For ten days your scorecard might add up to 8. Then the forecast was correct eight times out of ten, or 80 percent of the time. Not bad!

Are You Sure? Is It Impossible? Maybe!

"As a weatherman, you stink!" Danny said to Brian the next day.

"That was a hard call. Try me on something easier."

"OK. Will it snow on the Fourth of July?"

"No. Never." Brian was sure.

"How about Christmas?"

"Maybe."

"Will it rain Saturday afternoon?" Danny's father had promised to take the boys on a hike.

"Maybe."

"Wanna bet?"

"No." Brian was learning.

Danny turned on the TV so they could watch the ball game. No coin tossing this time. They were taking turns.

"If Missy comes in, I bet she'll grab the remote and change to *Sesame Street*. Wanna bet?"

"Sure . . . er . . . I mean no." Brian had lost a candy bar. He didn't want to lose anything more, for a while at least.

"What'll we watch now?" Brian asked when the game was over.

"Nothing," Danny answered. "We've got homework for Mrs. Abrams. She gave us a hard time about the math we didn't do. Remember?"

"Yeah, I know. Who cares? I'm going to do mine

when I get home." Brian switched channels to catch a monster show.

Danny opened his notebook and started reading. "Hey!" he said. "What's this? Everybody knows dinosaurs are extinct."

"Dinosaurs? Let me see." Brian turned off the TV and opened his notebook, too.

The worksheet that Mrs. Abrams, the boys' teacher, had given them is on the next page.

Danny and Brian marked their papers. *DO NOT MARK THIS BOOK.* Instead, take a piece of paper. On it write the numbers from 1 to 12. Read the directions. Then write *S*, *I*, or *M* after the number of each statement.

When you have finished, look on page 19 to find how Danny and Brian and the other students marked their papers. Do you agree? Why?

Directions:

Some things are *sure* to happen. If today is Monday, tomorrow will be Tuesday. Some things are *impossible*. You can't roll a seven with only one of a pair of dice. Some things may or may not happen. *Maybe* it will snow, *maybe* it won't.

Mark each of the following statements with *S* for sure, *I* for impossible, or *M* for maybe.

1 ★ There is a live dinosaur in the zoo.
2 ★ You will get tails if you toss a coin.
3 ★ It will rain on Saturday.
4 ★ Superman will always beat the bad guys.
5 ★ The next time you throw an ordinary ball, it will keep on going up into space.
6 ★ Someone will win a state lottery twice in one year.
7 ★ When you grow up, you will be ten feet tall.
8 ★ Outdoors at night you can see the stars in the sky.
9 ★ Your Little League team will win its next game.
10 ★ The earth revolves around the sun.
11 ★ You will be in school tomorrow.
12 ★ In a new box of crayons at least one will be red.

Maybe It's Impossible? For Sure!

Danny and Brian did not agree right away on how to mark all the items on the worksheet. Both put *I* in front of numbers 1, 5, and 7. They were easy. So was item 2. Brian had learned the hard way the chances of tails on a coin toss. Both boys marked it *M*. The boys also marked with *M* statements 3, 8, 9, and 11, but couldn't decide about 6. Brian marked it *I*. He was sure no one could ever win the lottery twice in one year. Danny remembered a news program he'd seen on TV. A lady had won the lottery twice in only four months. He marked it *M*. They marked with *S* numbers 10 and 12, also number 4 after they talked about it.

The next day the class discussed the probabilities of items 1 to 12 on the sheet. Most of the students agreed with Brian and Danny. One boy claimed his team was so bad it would never win, but the class convinced him it was possible. Another said that being in school tomorrow was impossible for him. His family would be leaving the night before for a long weekend. But a girl pointed out that their plans might change. And Mrs. Abrams suggested that the creator of Superman might one day decide to kill him off.

Brian and Danny shared their problem with 6, the one about winning the lottery.

"How many of you agree with Brian?" Mrs. Abrams wanted to know.

Almost all the students raised their hands.

"How many of you think Danny is right?"

Only Abigail put up her hand. Abigail's seat was in the center, right in front of Mrs. Abrams' desk.

"Why?" Mrs. Abrams asked her.

"I don't think it'll ever happen, someone winning the lottery twice, but that doesn't mean it's impossible," Abigail said.

Mrs. Abrams helped the students to understand how some events that seem impossible might take place. The chances that one person will win the lottery after buying a single ticket are often one in a million or more. Suppose there are about 250,000,000 people in the United States. Mathematicians claim there is a good chance that at least one of them will be a double winner at some time during his or her life. With numbers large enough, even the most unlikely events become possible.

Probability is determined by dividing what actually happens by the number of things that could happen, like this:

$$\text{Probability} = \frac{\text{what actually happens}}{\text{number of things that could happen}}$$

What are the chances that you will roll one, two, three, four, five, *or* six with a single die? There are six numbers from one to six. A die has six sides, numbered one through six. The probability of rolling one, two, three, four, five, *or* six with a single die is one (6/6 = 1). It is a sure thing.

Can you roll seven with a single die? You can't, because a single die shows only the numbers one through six. Only one side can be up at a time. The probability of such an impossible event is zero (0/6 = 0).

All events that aren't certain or impossible fall between one and zero, so their probabilities are expressed as fractions. When you toss a coin, it can land heads up or tails up. There are two possibilities, but only one actually happens. The probability is 1/2.

Probabilities can also be expressed as percentages. The probability of a certain event is 100 percent. The chances of getting heads or tails when tossing a single coin are 50 percent (1/2 = .50 = 50%).

When the chances that something will happen are more than 50 percent, we say it is probable, or likely, to happen. When they are less than 50 percent, the event is improbable, or unlikely.

Now You Try It: Is It Possible?

Make your own list of events that are sure to happen, might happen, or would never happen. For fun ask your friends and family to rate them as sure, possible, or impossible. Then ask: If something is neither sure to happen nor impossible, is it likely or unlikely? Why?

The ABC's of Probability

The Mysterious Message

It was quiet in Mrs. Abrams' classroom. The students were writing as their teacher moved up and down the rows. She bent over a desk to look at a student's paper.

Brian poked Danny in the middle of his back. "Psst . . . Danny," he whispered. As Danny turned around, Brian held up a folded note with the name ABIGAIL written in big capital letters on the outside. Danny reached for the note to pass it down the row.

"Wait!" said Brian. "I want to look first." He opened the note. "Hey! It's just a bunch of numbers."

The boys were puzzled. They didn't notice Mrs. Abrams moving in their direction.

"What's this?" she asked as she picked up the note.

"Er . . . uh . . . it just landed on my desk," answered Brian. He pantomimed an object dropping out of the air.

"Very interesting," commented Mrs. Abrams, studying the unfolded piece of paper.

In the back of the room the girl who had written the note looked worried. Her face turned a rosy pink.

Mrs. Abrams copied the note on the blackboard:

20-8-9-19   3-12-1-19-19   9-19   19-15
2-15-18-9-14-7.   4-15-5-19   13-18-19
1-2-18-1-13-19   4-25-5   8-5-18   8-1-9-18?

"The person who wrote this note was clever enough to use a code. Does any of you know what it is?" She smiled as she looked hard at the girl in the back row and then at Abigail.

Abigail tried to smile back. She did not raise her hand.

"How do you go about figuring out a message in code?" Mrs. Abrams asked.

"Well . . ." Danny was thinking out loud. "I bet those numbers stand for letters of the alphabet."

"You're probably right," said Mrs. Abrams. "But how can you figure out which ones?"

Abigail raised her hand partway. She lowered it, then raised it again. "That's easy," she said. "Look for numbers that come up a lot. See if groups of numbers make any sort of pattern."

"Yeah," agreed Danny.

"Shall we try that on this note, Abigail?" Mrs. Abrams asked.

"No!" the girl in the back of the room called out before Abigail could say anything.

Mrs. Abrams erased the numbers she had written on the board. "The girls should not have been writing notes in class," she said, "but I don't want to embarrass them. Abigail is right," she continued. "It helps to look for frequently used letters or groups of letters in a coded message. It would also help to know which letters are used most often in English."

She began to hand out composition paper.

"Uh-oh," muttered Brian. "More work coming."

"Put your name at the top of your paper," Mrs. Abrams said. "Fold it in half so you have two columns. Starting in the left-hand column, write each letter of the alphabet, like this." Mrs. Abrams wrote the alphabet on the blackboard.

At the top of the board she wrote this sentence: "What

letters are used most often in English?" As the students watched, she made a tally mark for each letter in the sentence. This is what Danny and Brian and their classmates saw on the board:

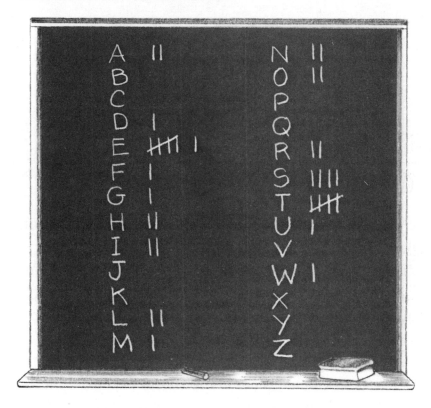

The class decided they would need to count the letters in much more than one word or a single sentence to get a fair idea of the frequency of letter usage in English. They would need a paragraph of several sentences. They took out their reading books. Each chose a paragraph. They began to mark their sheets. It was picky work. Brian kept forgetting to use a slanting tally mark for every fifth letter counted (卌). Then they worked in groups to list the letters used the most and the least.

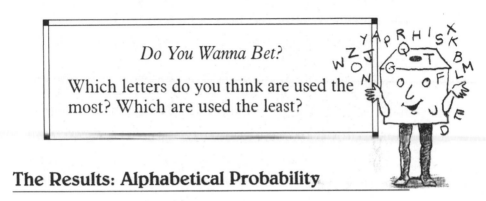

Do You Wanna Bet?

Which letters do you think are used the most? Which are used the least?

The Results: Alphabetical Probability

Brian helped Mrs. Abrams put the final totals on the board. E, A, T, O, and S were the letters most used. Other frequently used letters were I, N, and H. K, J, Q, and Z were used the least.

You weren't surprised, were you?

Now You Try It: Alphabetical Probability

1 ★ Choose a paragraph in a book or magazine. List the letters of the alphabet and use slash marks after each letter to tally the number of times it is used. Are your findings the same or different from those in Mrs. Abrams' class? How? Why?

2 ★ Do you play Scrabble®? Which letters have the most tiles? Which the fewest? Which are worth the most points? Is this a good arrangement? Why?

3 ★ Here is the Morse Code. It uses dots and dashes to send messages. Does it show the frequency of letter usage, or alphabetical probability, in English? How?

```
                MORSE CODE

    A  • —        J  • — — —      S  • • •
    B  — • • •     K  — • —       T  —
    C  — • — •     L  • — • •      U  • • —
    D  — • •      M  — —         V  • • • —
    E  •          N  — •         W  • — —
    F  • • — •     O  — — —       X  — • • —
    G  — — •      P  • — — •      Y  — • — —
    H  • • • •     Q  — — • —      Z  — — • •
    I  • •        R  • — •
```

Making and Breaking Codes

When Brian was back in his seat, he raised his hand. "What's all that got to do with codes?" he wanted to know.

"Can't you see?" Abigail responded. "The most-used letters, like E and A, S and T, are likely to appear in almost any word. And a one-letter word has to be A or I."

Danny's hand was in the air too. "Look for the symbol you see most often," he added. "That's probably going to stand for the letter E."

The students discussed codes they had used. Mrs. Abrams wrote some of them on the board.

Numbers: 1 for A, 2 for B, etc. to Z

or

26 for A, 25 for B, etc. to Z

Letters: Z for A, Y for B, etc.

or

B for A, C for B, etc.

Symbols: ∟ for A, ⌐ for B, ¬ for C, etc.

Such simple substitution codes are not hard, but the class decided that knowing letter-use frequency, or alphabetical probability, would help to break any of them.

"I used a simple number code to give you tomorrow's assignment," Mrs. Abrams said. "See if you can figure out what it is. I'll buy the first person who gets it right an ice cream in the lunchroom tomorrow." In the homework section of the blackboard Mrs. Abrams had written:

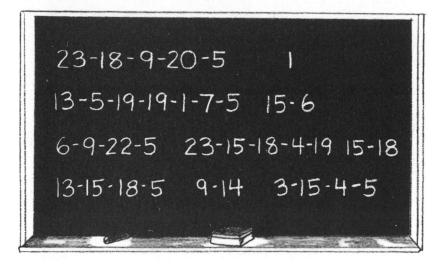

23-18-9-20-5   1

13-5-19-19-1-7-5   15-6

6-9-22-5   23-15-18-4-19   15-18

13-15-18-5   9-14   3-15-4-5

Do You Wanna Bet?

What was the assignment Mrs. Abrams wrote on the blackboard? Which code did she use? Who won the ice cream?

The Assignment

The assignment was: WRITE A MESSAGE OF FIVE WORDS OR MORE IN CODE. It was written in number code: 1 for A, 2 for B, etc. No one was surprised when Abigail won the ice cream.

The next day Danny gave his message to Brian to decode. Can you decode it? What code did Danny use?

G-S-V-I-V   R-H   Z   W-R-M-L-H-Z-F-I
R-M   G-S-V   Y-Z-H-V-N-V-M-G

Brian gave his to Danny. What was it? What code did he use?

14-9-8   26-25-9-26-14-8   18-8   26
4-18-22-9-23   7-22-26-24-19-22-9

☞ The decoded messages are on the next page.

The Messages

Danny used a reverse-letter code (Z for A, etc.) to write this message: THERE IS A DINOSAUR IN THE BASEMENT.

Brian used a reverse number code to write this message: MRS. ABRAMS IS A WIERD TEACHER. When Mrs. Abrams asked him to put his message on the board for the whole class to decode, he was embarrassed. He felt even worse when Abigail raised her hand. "The next-to-last word should be written 4-22-18-9-23," she said. Brian had misspelled WEIRD.

Now You Try It: Making and Breaking Codes

1 ★ Write a message in code to exchange with a friend. Use your knowledge of letter frequency in English to break your friend's code and read the message.

"Swip mish be dimble frop"? That can't be the message.

2 ★ At your next party hide a treasure somewhere in your house or outdoors. Write a message in code that tells where to find it. The first person to decode the message and find the treasure gets to keep it.

3 ★ Decode the message on page 26 Mrs. Abrams erased from the board. Would the girls have minded if Mrs. Abrams had let the class decode it? What code did they use?

4 ★ The letter and number substitution codes used by Mrs. Abrams' students were easy to break. How could you change them to make them harder?

The secret message from page 24...

Birthday Party

Same Birthday

"You going to Jamie's party this Saturday?" Danny asked Brian at the bus stop Wednesday morning.

"I don't know," Brian answered.

"What do you mean, you don't know? Jamie always has great parties. His mother took us bowling last year. Don't you want to go bowling?"

"Sure I want to go bowling, but I got another invitation in the same mail."

"Another invitation? Who from?"

"Mark."

"Mark Andrews?"

"Yeah."

"I don't believe it. Two kids in our class can't have their birthdays on the same day," Danny said. "That's impossible."

"I'm talking about parties, not birthdays. Your party doesn't have to be on your exact birthday."

"OK, OK, so Mark's having a birthday party on Saturday. He's a jerk. He didn't invite me, so I won't be there. You won't have any fun."

"Says who? Anyway, I opened Mark's invitation first, and my mom says I have to go to his party. His mom and my mom are friends. What am I going to do?"

"Just tell her the truth. Jamie's party will be more fun. You know it will. And I'll be there. Your mom likes me. She says I'm a good influence."

"Hah!" said Brian, but he added, "OK, I'll try."

Mrs. Abrams always began class with a question-and-answer period. She called it "What's on Your Mind?" The students asked questions. Other students tried to answer them. If they couldn't, Mrs. Abrams helped. Sometimes a student had to go to the library to find the answer.

This morning Danny raised his hand. "Mrs. Abrams, can two kids in one class have the same birthday? Is it possible?"

"Sure it's possible," she said.

"How about this class?" Danny asked.

Mrs. Abrams took her attendance book out of her desk and opened it. "Let me see." She ran her finger down the list of students. "Mark and Jamie have the same birthday. It's this coming Saturday."

"See?" Brian nudged Danny.

But Danny wasn't satisfied. "That's just a weird coincidence," he said. "I bet this is the only class in this school with two kids who have the same birthday."

"Who agrees with Danny?" Mrs. Abrams asked.

Almost all the students raised their hands. Danny looked pleased, but Abigail objected. "I think we should check it out," she said. "I bet there'll be another one in the twelve classes in this school, maybe more."

"OK," Mrs. Abrams agreed. "I'll give you a note to take to the principal. His secretary can look over the class lists for us. And we'll all celebrate for Mark and Jamie on Friday."

Do You Wanna Bet?

Is there another class in the school with two students who have the same birthday? Maybe two or three? What are the chances?

The Chances: Same Birthday

Danny was wrong. Abigail was right. When the school secretary checked the class lists, she found that in four of the twelve classes in the school there were two children with the same birthday. But the students in Mrs. Abrams' class were not convinced until the secretary came to their room to show them.

And they didn't want to believe Mrs. Abrams when she explained the chances: In any group of twenty-three people, there is a better than 50 percent chance that at least two will have the same birthday.

Sometimes it is easier to discover the probability of an event by first figuring out the chances that it *won't* happen. Suppose you have twenty-three friends who might invite you to their birthday parties. The first person can have any birthday at all. What are the chances that the second person has a *different* birthday? They are 364 out of 365 (364/365), since the first person has used up one day of the year. For the third person, the chances are 363/365, since two days of the year have been used. If you continue with this process, the probability for the twenty-third person is 365 minus 22, which equals 343, divided by 365—or 343/365. Multiply all the probabilities, as you would for multiple coin tosses, to get .49, or 49 percent. There are forty-nine chances in one hundred that no two of your friends will have the same birthday. This means there are fifty-one chances in one hundred that two or more will.

Danny bet Mrs. Abrams that no one in the school shared his birthday. He won, even though there were 315 students in the school. The chances of finding someone born on your particular birthday are smaller than those of finding at least two people who share a birthday.

Now You Try It: Same Birthday

Take a survey of your friends, your school class, all the classes in your school. Ask people their birthdays. Stop when you find two with the same one.

When Danny tried it, he felt like giving up. He had to ask thirty-two people before he found two with the same birthday. Abigail was luckier. She found two people with the same birthday after asking only twelve.

Door Prize

When Danny arrived at Jamie's house Saturday afternoon, he was surprised to see Brian.

"How come you didn't have to go to Mark's?" he asked.

"Easy. Wednesday night I cleared the table *and* loaded the dishwasher. I took out the garbage. I did *all* my chores without being told. When I asked Mom if I could go to Jamie's instead of Mark's, she had to say yes."

"Smart thinking," said Danny.

Jamie had handed each boy a number as he arrived at the party. The numbers were for the door prize.

"What number have you got?" Brian asked Danny.

"I've got eleven. What's yours?"

"Seven," Brian answered. "That's lucky. I know I'm going to win the prize."

"That's what you think. I've got as good a chance as you have," Danny said.

Do You Wanna Bet?

Was Danny right? Were his chances as good as Brian's? Jamie had handed a number from one to eleven to each of his eleven guests. What chance did each boy have of winning the prize?

The Boys' Chances: Door Prize

Danny's chances were as good as Brian's. With eleven boys, eleven numbers, and one prize, each boy had one chance in eleven of winning it (1/11).

The number seven was not lucky for Brian. Jamie's cousin from a nearby town won the door prize, but Brian and Danny didn't care. It was a book about probability. They had a great time bowling.

How Many Red? Brown? Yellow?

When the boys returned from the bowling alley, Jamie's mother handed out prizes for the best scores. Danny just missed getting third. Then they sat down at the dining-room table for refreshments. There was no food on the table.

"I'm starving! You told me that last year Jamie's mother took you out for hot dogs and hamburgers," Brian complained to Danny. "Mark's party was going to McDonald's for lunch. I wish I'd gone to Mark's."

"Shhh . . ." Danny asked Brian to be quiet as Jamie's mother put a small cannister on the table. She told them it was filled with color-coated chocolate candies.

"Is that all we're going to get to eat?" Brian whispered.

Danny shushed him again.

At each boy's place was a piece of paper with his name on it. Underneath were listed the colors red, brown, and yellow.

"What's this for?" one boy asked.

"I'm about to tell you," Jamie's mother promised. "In this cannister are three hundred candies. Some are red, some are brown, some are yellow. You have to guess how many there are of each color. You will have three chances to figure out the correct totals—one after ten have been taken out of the cannister, another after twenty, and the last after thirty. The boy with the answer that comes closest to the real totals will win this prize." She held up a solar-powered calculator. "Jamie helped me set this up, so he's going to pick out the candies."

She shook the cannister to mix the candies. "Jamie," she requested, "without looking, take ten candies out of the cannister." She held it so he couldn't see the colors. Jamie took out ten candies.

"How many do you have of each color?" his mother asked.

"I have five red, three brown, and two yellow," Jamie answered. He put the candies down on the table.

"Now make your first estimate," his mother told the boys. "Remember that your total should be three

hundred. And don't let anyone see your paper. No copying."

"This is just like school." Brian was complaining again.

"Of course it is," said Danny. "Jamie's mother is a math teacher at Cranbrook Middle School. Didn't you know that?"

She did sound like a teacher. "How many red candies do you think are in the cannister?" she asked.

"A hundred and fifty," Danny answered quickly. Half the candies Jamie took out were red, so half of the three hundred in the cannister should be red too, he thought.

"What about yellow?"

"Sixty," said the boy at the end of the table.

"And brown?"

Danny added 60 to 150 to get 210, then subtracted 210 from 300. "Ninety," he said.

"Good thinking, but maybe you'll change your mind after we've taken out more candies," said Jamie's mother.

Jamie took out ten more. The boys tried again. The third time he called out the final totals for the colors: nine red, seventeen brown, and four yellow.

"Now make your final estimate of the total number of each color," directed Jamie's mother.

The boys sputtered and complained, but they all wrote down something before she collected the slips.

Do You Wanna Bet?

How many candies of each color—red, brown, and yellow—were in the cannister at Jamie's birthday party?

A Sample: How Big Should It Be?

Of the 300 candies in the cannister, 100 were red, 150 were brown, and 50 were yellow. How close did you come?

Danny took the total of candies sampled (30), divided it into 300, and got 10, or 10 percent of the 300 candies in the cannister. He multiplied the total for each color in the candies sampled by 10 and got 90 red, 170 brown, and 40 yellow. Jamie's cousin and another boy had the same numbers. All three won prizes.

You remember that after the first sampling of only ten candies, the boys thought there were 150 red, 90 brown, and 60 yellow. Their totals were closer with the second sampling, closest with the third. They learned that the larger the sample you take, the closer you will come to getting the right numbers.

Jamie's mother was a good teacher, but a birthday party is not the place for lessons. She quickly served large portions of pizza and then ice cream cake, and gave each boy two small bags of candies. They forgot all about math and had a good time.

Now You Try It: Sampling

1 ★ Set up a sampling experiment like the one Jamie's mother arranged for his birthday party. You don't need candies. You can use poker chips, colored beads, even painted pennies or bottle caps. There

should be a large number, at least one hundred. Count the number there are of each color. Then place all the items in a paper bag or other container that will hide the colors. Shake until the items are well mixed. Tell a friend or member of your family the total number of items and what colors they are but not how many there are of each color. Ask your helper to take out a small number—five or ten, for example—from the container, then try to estimate how many of each color there are all together. Have your helper try again after taking out a larger number. How large a sample did you need to make an estimate that came close to the right total?

2 ★ Sampling can also be used to find out the total number of items in a container without counting each one. To try it, fill a container with pieces of macaroni. Remove a handful of pieces. Count them. Color them with a marker. Then return them to the container. Shake it several times to mix the pieces. Remove another handful. This time count both the number of marked pieces and the *total* number of pieces in the handful.

Suppose there were twenty-four pieces in the first handful, which you marked and put back in the container. There are thirty pieces in the second handful. Four of them are marked. How will you estimate the total number of pieces in the container?

Your second handful contains four of the twenty-four marked pieces, or one-sixth of them ($4/24 = 1/6$).

PLAIN	MARKED
11	2

Chances are you also have about one-sixth of the unmarked ones. If you multiply 30, the number of pieces in the second handful, by 6, you get 180, an *estimate* of the total number of pieces in the container.

Now count the items in the container. How close did your estimate come to the total? (Be sure to throw away the pieces afterward so no one eats them!)

Wildlife managers sometimes use a sampling method like this to estimate the number of fish in a pond. Would sampling be a good way to estimate the number of people in the United States? Some experts think this method should be considered by U.S. census takers.

Sampling and Statistics

Left Hand or Right?

"Get your elbow out of my way," Brian said to Danny, who was sitting at his right at a crowded table in the school library. "How can I take notes when you keep hitting my arm?"

"I can't help it. *You* move over," Danny said. "I'm left-handed. Remember?"

"Yeah, you're a lefty. You're weird."

"Nah! Lots of people write with their left hands." Danny defended himself.

"Who says?"

"*I* say!"

Mrs. Abrams overheard the boys' conversation. "Be quiet," she told them. "We'll talk about this when we're through in the library."

Back in the classroom Mrs. Abrams waited for the students to settle down. "Brian just called Danny weird because he writes with his left hand. Is that fair?" she asked.

"It's fair to call Danny weird because he *is* weird," Brian said.

"Is writing left-handed as strange as all that?" Mrs. Abrams wanted to know.

"It depends," said Abigail, "on how many other people write with their left hands."

"How many students in this school write left-handed?" Mrs. Abrams asked.

Brian raised his hand. "I don't think there're more than five," he said.

"Why?"

"Just guessing," Brian mumbled.

Other students suggested ten, fifteen, twenty before Mrs. Abrams told them to stop guessing. "How would you go about finding out how many left-handed writers there are?" she asked.

"I'd ask the school secretary," one girl suggested.

"She wouldn't know. I'd ask the nurse," said a boy.

"She won't know either. I'd ask all the teachers to poll the students in their classes," said Abigail.

"They might not want to be bothered," said Mrs. Abrams. "Let's start with this class. Who writes left-handed?"

It turned out that two students besides Danny in Mrs. Abrams' class wrote left-handed. "Think about it," she said. "You know there are three left-handed writers in this class. You know there are twelve classes in the school. How many left-handed writers do you think there are?"

Do You Wanna Bet?

How would you answer Mrs. Abrams' question? How many left-handed writers were there in Brian and Danny's school?

Taking a Sample: Left-Handedness

The boys and girls in Mrs. Abrams' class were pretty smart. It took them only a moment to multiply 3 students by 12 classes to get a total of 36 as their estimate of the number of left-handed writers in the school.

It took much longer to get the eleven other teachers to check with their classes. The students found that there actually were twenty-nine left-handed writers in the school.

From research in the school library Abigail reported that about one person in every ten writes left-handed. Brian and Danny decided that she probably spent her spare time reading encyclopedias.

Baseball Statistics and Strategy

Danny and Brian could not believe their eyes. Coming toward the bench where they were sitting was a girl. She had on a gray sweatshirt with TOMCATS written in big bright-orange letters across the front. That was the name of their Little League team. When she moved closer, they saw it was Abigail.

"Hi, guys!" she said.

"What're you doing here?" Danny asked.

"Yeah. Go sit in the stands. Get lost," Brian added before she could answer.

"No way. My dad said I could sit here."

"Who's your dad?"

"You don't know who my dad is? You're kidding!"

Brian and Danny thought for a moment. Uh-oh. Abigail Farnsworth. Mr. Farnsworth was their coach.

"Um . . . yeah . . . we know," Danny said. "But what are you doing on the bench?"

"My dad just made me team statistician. I'm going to figure out the batting averages, stuff like that."

Brian and Danny didn't say anything. They were thinking. Finally Danny asked, "Can you tell us who's going to win today?"

"Well . . ." Abigail answered slowly. She looked down at her clipboard. "Last year the Eagles played twelve games. They won seven and lost five. Their percentage of wins was fifty-eight. The Tomcats won only four out of twelve. Their percentage was thirty-three. The Eagles are sure to beat you."

"No they aren't!" Danny protested. "You can't use last year's figures to predict what's going to happen today! They've got lots of new players. So have we. Ours could be better than theirs."

"I have to use last year's figures," Abigail said. "You haven't played yet this season. Neither have the Eagles."

Abigail was busy writing on her clipboard when her dad arrived to assign positions and set up the batting order for the day's game.

Neither of the boys approved of the batting order. "How come Joe is batting fourth this time?" Danny asked Brian.

Before he could answer, Abigail spoke up. "Didn't you know? Joe's got the highest batting average of anyone on the team. Last year he batted four hundred."

"That's impossible," Brian said. "Nobody on this team's that good."

"You're right. We're not. Joe hardly got a hit in practice. Where'd you get that average?" Danny asked Abigail.

"I divided the number of hits by the number of times at bat. It came out four hundred. I'll show you. Look!" She opened to a page in the team notebook.

"Aha!" Danny pointed to her figures: 4 hits in 10 times at bat. "That's it," he said. "I remember now. Joe hurt his wrist last year. He played in only the first three or four games. It's stupid to put him in the cleanup spot."

"Don't call my dad stupid!" Abigail said. "Just you wait and see. I bet Joe gets a home run."

Do You Wanna Bet?

Will Joe get a home run? Will the Tomcats win the game? What kind of season will they have? How helpful are baseball statistics in setting up the batting order and predicting the success of a particular team?

Baseball Statistics and Strategy

Joe did get a home run, but no one was on base and the Tomcats lost the game. Brian and Danny told Abigail she was bad luck for everyone but Joe. They were worried about the upcoming season. With her as statistician, they were sure their opponents would have an advantage.

Statistics play an important part in baseball strategy—how coaches and managers plan to win games. However, it is always important to consider the figures on which they are based. Joe's batting average the previous season was .400 for ten times at bat. If he had played the entire season of twelve games, he would probably have been at bat about thirty-five times. It is unlikely he could have maintained his opening hitting streak that long even if he is a good hitter.

Also, players are not machines. They have good days and bad days. Not everything should go by the numbers.

Now You Try It: Baseball Statistics and Strategy

1 ★ Pretend you are the statistician for a real baseball team. Keep a record of its wins and losses. Figure out its percentage of wins by dividing the number of wins by the number of games played. Compare this year's percentage with last year's. How do you think the team will do next season? Predict its percentage, then check against the number of wins and losses in the games played.

2 ★ If you play on a baseball team, figure out your batting average by dividing the total of hits you've made by the total number of times at bat. Do this for your friends and other members of your team after each game and at the end of the season. Are there any surprises? If there are, what might explain them?

3 ★ Pretend you are the manager of a baseball team. Two of your players have the same .300 batting average. The first player has hit in 3 out of 10 times at bat. The second player has hit in 30 out of 100 times. Which player would you choose as your cleanup hitter? Why?

PTA Carnival

Take a Chance! Win a TV Set!

"I bet I've sold more raffle tickets than you have," Brian said to Danny. The boys were walking home from the bus stop the week before the PTA carnival.

"I bet you have, too," Danny agreed. "I hate to ask people to buy things."

"You're a wimp," said Brian. "I just walk up and down the street ringing doorbells. It's easy. Some of the people say no, but most buy at least one ticket for a dollar. I smile and say thank you. They think I'm cute."

"Cute? They're crazy!"

"Maybe, but I sold fifteen chances just on Vineyard. How many did you sell?"

"Only twelve so far. I just asked my parents and my grandma. My dad took some to the place where he works. Maybe his friends will buy them."

"How many did your parents take?"

"Ten."

"Wow! Why'd they buy so many?"

"They're tired of hearing Missy and me argue about the TV. They really want another set. And they want to help out the PTA, too."

"Think they'll win?"

"I don't know. If they do, Missy can watch her show and we can watch ours. She won't bug us anymore."

"Yeah, but I really want that TV, too. I'm going to spend five dollars I've got saved for chances for myself. If I win, we can watch in *my* room at *my* house. No Missy there."

Do You Wanna Bet?

What were the chances that Danny's parents would win the TV set? What were Brian's chances? What do you need to know besides how many raffle tickets each bought?

The Chances: PTA Raffle

You need to know the total number of tickets sold to figure anyone's chances of winning the prize. Divide the number of chances bought by any one person by the total number sold, like this:

$$\text{Probability of winning} = \frac{\text{chances bought}}{\text{total chances sold}}$$

If two thousand tickets were sold, Danny's parents would have one chance in two hundred of winning with their tickets (10/2,000 = 1/200). With his five tickets Brian would have one chance in four hundred (5/2,000 = 1/400). Danny's parents' chances would be twice as good as Brian's.

☞ Read to the end of this chapter to find out who won the raffle.

Lucky Wheel

Brian and Danny crossed the school parking lot on the morning of the PTA carnival. Brian was sure he was going to win the TV set. Danny hoped his parents would. Bright sunshine made the playground glisten as the boys walked along the row of booths to see what was going on.

In one booth they could be made up to look like clowns, monsters, or Indians. "Missy would like that," Danny said, but they decided it was kid stuff, not worth their money.

In another they could throw balls at a target to win a pink teddy bear. Danny had a good arm, but the prizes looked cheap. Even Missy wouldn't want one, in Danny's opinion.

They stopped at the last booth under a big sign that read LUCKY WHEEL. This was more like it. A large wheel was divided into equal sections numbered from 1 to 10 on the outside edge. It cost only a quarter to play, five tries for a dollar.

"Step right up!" called the man with the mustache who was running the booth. "Watch the wheel turn! Spend a quarter! Win a dollar!"

"Hey, this is great," said Brian. "How can I lose?"

"I know you. You can," said Danny.

Brian paid no attention. He put a dollar on the counter.

"What number do you want?" the man asked.

"Seven. That's my lucky number," Brian replied.

The man gave Brian a card with a 7 on it. "Step right up, boys and girls!" he shouted. "Spend a quarter! Win a dollar!"

A couple of kids took numbers 8 and 10. Another took 3.

"C'mon, Danny," Brian urged his friend. "Take a number."

"I want to see how it works first."

Finally the man spun the wheel. Fast it went, round and round. Then it slowed, almost stopped . . . 2, 3, 4, 5 . . . Brian held his breath . . . 6. It stopped at 6. No one had bet on 6.

"Ohhh," Brian groaned. "They should grease that wheel."

The other kids had bet a quarter. They walked away. More boys and girls came up. The man took their quarters and gave them cards with the numbers they chose.

"What's your bet this time, fella?" he asked Brian, who had four more chances. "You going to stick with seven?"

"Yeah," Brian said.

"Why don't you try another number?" asked Danny.

"Seven's lucky for me," Brian replied.

"Sure. That's why you won last time," Danny said.

Do You Wanna Bet?

What were Brian's chances of winning on the Lucky Wheel? Would the number seven be lucky for him? Was the Lucky Wheel a good way for the PTA to make money?

The Chances: Lucky Wheel

The spaces on the Lucky Wheel were numbered from 1 to 10. Each time Brian chose a number and the wheel spun, he had one chance in ten of winning a dollar. Each chance cost him twenty cents, because he had bought five chances for a dollar. For him to come out ahead, the wheel would have had to stop on his number on more than one spin out of five.

It didn't. Brian bet on 7 each time. Each time the wheel stopped on another number. One kid did win a dollar on the number 2, another on 5, a third on 1. Brian was angry because he didn't win anything for his dollar and those kids won dollars for their quarters. They had "beginner's luck." It doesn't last forever. The more often you bet, the less likely you are to win in the long run.

The PTA couldn't lose on the Lucky Wheel, but didn't make a lot of money either. If bets were placed on all the numbers at twenty-five cents each, the man in charge would take in $2.50 on each spin. The most he would have to pay out would be $1.00. He'd have $1.50 left for the PTA.

However, some kids, like Brian, bought five chances for a dollar. And most of the time the man in charge didn't wait to spin until all the numbers had been taken. The raffle, not the Lucky Wheel, was the big money-maker at the carnival.

Now You Try It: Lucky Wheel

For your own Lucky Wheel, use the spinner from a game you have, or make one by using cardboard for the base and pointer with a paper fastener to hold them together. You may use colors or designs instead of numbers. For the wheel to be fair, the sections must be exactly equal and the pointer must move freely.

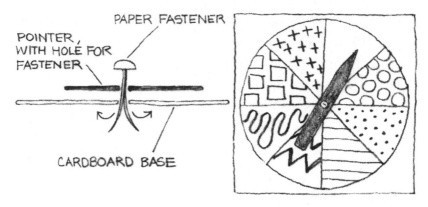

Choose a number, color, or design. Estimate how often the spinner will stop on it in ten spins. Spin the spinner ten times. Use tally marks to keep a record of where it stops each time. How close was your estimate? Try again with more spins. On each spin your chance of getting your chosen number, color, or design is one divided by the total number of sections on the wheel. The more often you spin, the easier it will be to see that this is true.

Spin the wheel at your next party or at a fund-raiser. Have prizes for the people who win.

Guessing the Colors

"What are you waiting for? Why don't you spend some money?" Brian asked Danny.

"If I spend money, I want to get something for it," Danny answered. He was thinking of how Brian had lost five times in a row on the Lucky Wheel.

The boys had bought candy bars and had sodas to drink before they saw the fifth-grade booth. It was decorated in red, white, and blue. The girl in the booth was running a guessing game.

"C'mon guys, you can be a winner," she told the boys. "See these?" She pointed to three cards lying facedown on the counter in front of her. "One is red underneath, one is white, and one is blue. Guess which is which and you win a dollar." She turned the cards over to show the boys. Then she turned them facedown again and moved them around quickly. "Want to guess?"

"How much?" Danny asked.

"One chance for a quarter. Five chances for a dollar. You look like smart guys. C'mon, take a chance," she urged.

"OK, I'll take five." Danny gave her a dollar.

Brian could hardly believe his eyes and ears. "How come you're taking a chance this time?" he asked.

"I think I can figure out what she's doing with the cards," Danny said.

"You got x-ray vision?" Brian wanted to know. "The backs of the cards look all the same to me."

"I can't see through the cards, but I've been watching her hands. Red on the left, then blue, then white," he guessed.

The girl turned over the cards. They showed blue, red, white, left to right.

"Tough luck," Brian said to Danny. He gave the girl a big smile.

She smiled back, then moved the cards around quickly. "Guess again," she said.

Danny did.

Do You Wanna Bet?

What were Danny's chances of guessing the correct order of the face-down cards? Did he get it right on any of his five tries? Was this a good way for the fifth graders to make money for the PTA? Who won the PTA raffle?

Danny's Chances: Guessing the Colors

The colored cards the girl was using could be placed in six different orders. On each guess Danny had one chance in six (1/6) of having the order correct.

With five guesses for a dollar, he had paid only twenty cents for each guess. He tried to follow the girl's hands as she moved the cards around. She was too quick for him most of the time, but he won a dollar on his last guess. While he didn't make any money, he didn't lose any either. He broke even.

At this game a player had one chance in six of winning. Although the fifth graders charged a quarter a guess, or a dollar for five guesses, they paid out a dollar each time someone guessed right. They did not make as much money as the Lucky Wheel, where a player's chances of winning were only one in ten.

Neither Brian nor Danny's parents won the TV. Abigail, the girl who always had the right answers, won the raffle. She wasn't just brainy. She was lucky, too. Unfair.

Now You Try It: Guessing the Colors

1 ★ Use one red, one white, and one blue poker chip (or colored slips of paper) to check the chances of winning at the fifth-grade booth. See how many different combinations you can make. Write them down using R (for red), W (for white), B (for blue). Did you get six?

2 ★ What would the chances be with two colors? Or if a fourth color were added? Use chips or homemade cards to discover the number of different arrangements

you can make with four colors. Did you think there would be so many?

3 ★ Make your own set of three color cards. Be sure the backs of the cards are exactly alike. Or use three playing cards. Have your friends guess the order of the cards. Maybe some of them have x-ray vision.

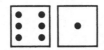

Winners and Losers

Playing Cards

"Why doesn't it stop raining?" Brian asked Danny.

"It knows you want it to. It's out to get you," Danny replied.

The boys had been indoors all that Saturday. Their Little League game had been rescheduled. The baseball game on TV was rained out, too.

"What're we going to do now?" Danny asked his father, who had just come into the den.

"Why don't you play cards?" he suggested.

"OK," the boys agreed, but they were not very enthusiastic. They took a long time to set up the card table and find the cards.

They were just about ready to start when Missy appeared. "I want to play too," she said.

"Get lost, Missy. We're not playing Go Fish," Danny said.

"Hey, how about Fifty-two Pickup?" Brian suggested.

"What's that?" she asked.

"Look!" Brian said. He lifted the cards off the table. Then he riffled them in a wide arc. They fell to the floor. "You lose," he said. "You get to pick them all up."

Missy looked confused.

"That's the game. You wanted to play. There're fifty-two cards. You get to pick them all up yourself. Fifty-two Pickup!" Brian explained.

Missy's eyes filled with tears. She ran toward the stairs. "Daddy! Daddy!" she cried.

The boys picked up the cards as fast as they could. They knew Danny's father would be there in a minute, and he was. "Grow up, fellas," he said. "Give Missy a break."

After he left, Danny shuffled the deck loosely a couple of times. "Want to play rummy?" he asked.

"Why not?" Brian answered.

Danny dealt Brian and himself seven cards each. He put the rest of the pack facedown on the table, with one card faceup next to it.

Brian wanted to be the first to lay down his hand and "go rummy." So did Danny. To do this each needed *either* four of a kind (four eights or four queens, for example) and a sequence of three cards in order in the same suit (three, four, five of hearts, for example), *or* three of a kind and a four-card sequence.

Brian and Danny arranged their hands. Cards of the same kind went together. So did cards that made sequences in the same suit. Danny placed two sixes together and put the eight of hearts next to the nine. The rest of his cards did not match. Brian had two jacks, but the rest of his cards did not match at all.

"You start," Danny told Brian.

Brian studied his hand. He drew a six from the top of the face-down pile, then put it down on top of the card that was face-up.

Danny picked up Brian's six. He had a big smile on his face. "Your turn," he said as he pulled the five of clubs from his hand and put it on the face-up pile.

Brian was sorry he had given Danny something he could use. He picked again from the face-down pile, looked at his hand, and discarded. The card he put down was the ten of hearts.

"Aha!" said Danny. "Just what I wanted." He quickly picked up the ten and rearranged his cards.

"You cheated," Brian complained. "You had to cheat to pick up two cards in a row like that. You're going to win. It's because you dealt. You put the cards where you wanted them."

"C'mon, lay off me," Danny said. "Would I cheat you? You're my best friend. Besides, I bet you'll win anyway."

Do You Wanna Bet?

Is luck all that matters in a game like rummy? Is there anything players can do to improve their chances? What is the probability of being dealt a particular card? How often should the cards be shuffled to be sure they are not in any special order? Did Brian win the game?

The Chances: Playing Cards

When Danny picked up his hand, he already had two sixes and the eight and nine of hearts. He was lucky to begin with, and lucky again because Brian discarded the cards that he needed.

The probability of drawing any particular card from a full deck—the ace of spades, for example—is one out of fifty-two (1/52). There are thirteen cards in each of the four suits in the deck of fifty-two cards. The probability of drawing a card of a particular kind from a full deck—a two, ten, or queen, for example—is one out of thirteen. There are four of each kind, and 4/52 = 1/13.

It is twice as easy to fill in at either end of a sequence of cards in order than to fill in the card missing in the middle. In his game with Brian, Danny had the eight and nine of hearts. To make a three-card sequence, he could have used either a seven or a ten (7, 8, 9, 10). Suppose he had been dealt the seven and nine of hearts instead of the eight and nine. To complete that sequence, he would have had to get an eight (7, 8, 9).

Danny did not cheat, but Brian was right to complain about Danny's shuffling. A deck should be shuffled at least a half dozen times to be sure the cards are not in any special order.

Danny very quickly had three sixes and the eight, nine, and ten of hearts. To complete his hand, however, he could use only one of three cards—another six, or the seven or jack of hearts. And Brian's luck changed. He picked up cards that he could use. He was able to lay down his hand and "go rummy" before Danny.

Now You Try It: Playing Cards

1 ★ There are four suits in a deck of playing cards: clubs, diamonds, hearts, and spades. There are thirteen cards in each suit: two, three, four, five, six, seven, eight, nine, ten, jack, queen, king, ace. Separate the suits and put the cards in order in each suit. Then shuffle the deck once. How much did the order change? Check again after two shuffles, then three, four, five. How many times did you have to shuffle the deck to mix the cards thoroughly?

When the cards have been shuffled seven times, deal
five hands of ten cards each. How many hands contain
two of a kind? How many contain three of a kind? Are
there any sequences (cards of the same suit in order)?
Repeat this experiment several times. Use tally marks
to keep a record of the results of each deal. Are they the
same or different? How different are they?

2 ★ Luck plays a role in all card games, but you can
improve your chances the next time you play if you remember the probabilities. Some combinations of cards
are more likely to turn up than others. It is easier to
complete a sequence at one end or the other than in the
middle. It also helps to pay attention. Remember the
cards that have been played. Don't expect them to turn
up again. Try not to discard the cards you think your
opponent wants. Some players like to bluff—try to fool
the people they play against. This may work, but not if
they do it too often. Above all, don't cheat.

Roll of the Dice

Danny wasn't happy that Brian had won the game of
rummy. "You're just lucky," he complained. "I bet I
can beat you in Monopoly®. That takes skill."

"Nah. It's all in the roll of the dice," Brian said.
"C'mon, I'll show you. This is my lucky day."

It was still raining, so the boys put away the playing

cards and got out the Monopoly® board. In a few minutes they had divided and counted their money. They were ready to go into the real-estate business in Atlantic City.

Soon after they'd started playing, Danny had a chance to buy Boardwalk. "I'll take it," he said. It was early in the game. Even though Boardwalk cost a lot, he had the money to pay for it. "You're going to owe me rent. Just wait till I put some hotels on it," he said to Brian. "I'm going to get you."

"Who says?" Brian didn't believe it. He used his money to buy the orange properties: St. James Place, Tennessee Avenue, and New York Avenue. He put hotels on them as soon as he had a chance. "I'm going to win this game," he told Danny. He rolled a seven and missed landing on Boardwalk.

Do You Wanna Bet?

Did Brian win? If he did, was it because he was lucky or because he was smart? What are the chances of rolling any given number, one through six, with a single die? Two through twelve with a pair of dice? And what are the chances of rolling a double, which gives an extra turn in Monopoly®?

The Chances: Roll of the Dice

Brian was lucky when he rolled the dice and missed Boardwalk and Park Place, which Danny had bought when he landed on it. Also Brian was smart to buy the orange properties—St. James Place, Tennessee Avenue, and New York Avenue. Their rent, even with hotels, is not as high as that for Danny's blue properties, but the orange properties are not far beyond the space marking Jail. In Monopoly® a player is likely to have to go to Jail. Danny did, and he landed on Brian's properties when he got out. Brian won the game.

A die has six faces, so the chances of rolling any given number, one through six, with a single die are one out of six (1/6).

Rolling a pair of dice is like tossing two coins at the same time. What happens to the second die does not depend on what happens to the first. To roll a given number on the first die, the chances are one out of six (1/6). For the second die they are also one out of six (1/6). Multiply 1/6 by 1/6 to get 1/36. There are thirty-six possible outcomes with a pair of dice.

The chances of rolling any given number from two to twelve with a pair of dice depend on how many different ways there are of rolling that number. For Brian's lucky number, seven, there are six ways: 1–6, 2–5, 3–4, 4–3, 5–2, 6–1. The probability of each is 1/36. Adding 1/36 + 1/36 + 1/36 + 1/36 + 1/36 + 1/36 gives a total of 6/36 or 1/6, the chances of rolling a seven with a pair of dice. Only two possible combinations will give a sum of three, 1–2 and 2–1, so the chances of rolling a three are 1/36 + 1/36 = 2/36, or 1/18.

To roll a double with a pair of dice, six combinations are possible: 1–1, 2–2, 3–3, 4–4, 5–5, 6–6. For each, the chances are one out of thirty-six (1/36). Add 1/36 + 1/36 + 1/36 + 1/36 + 1/36 + 1/36 to get a total of 6/36, or 1/6. The chances of rolling any double are one out of six.

Now You Try It: Roll of the Dice

1 ★ Conduct your own experiment to check the chances of rolling a given number with one die. Make a tally sheet like this (*DO NOT MARK THIS BOOK!*):

```
I.      4.
2.      5.
3.      6.
```

Roll a die. Put a tally mark after the number on your sheet that matches the number on the side that is up. Do this ten times. Did you get at least one tally mark for each number? Roll the die one hundred times. Your total for each number should not be too far from 16 or 17 (1/6 × 100).

2 ★ Do doubles really turn up on the average of one roll in six with a pair of dice? Experiment by keeping a record with tally marks for one hundred throws. How close does your total come to 1/6 × 100?

DIE	COIN
1	H
6	T
3	H
4	H
2	T
2	T
6	T
1	H

3 ★ Figure the chances of getting any of the other possible totals besides seven or three by rolling a pair of dice. Seven is the most likely to turn up. Which are the least likely? Seeing the possible combinations is easier if you use dice of different colors—one red and one green, for example.

4 ★ Roll a die and toss a coin at the same time. What are the chances of throwing a six on the die at the same time that the coin lands heads up? Use tally marks to keep track of your tries, with H for heads and T for tails for the coin, and the numbers 1 through 6 for the die. How many times did you roll and toss before a six and heads appeared together once? A second time? A third?

The chances of rolling a six on the die are 1/6. The chances of getting heads on the coin are 1/2. Multiply 1/6 by 1/2 to get 1/12, the chances of rolling a six at the same time a coin lands heads up.

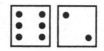

Last Chance

What Shall We Name the Baby?

Danny's mother's face was wet with perspiration. "It's hot out there," she said, pointing to the kitchen. "And I have a little furnace right here," she added, patting her big tummy. "Your little brother or sister is keeping me warm."

She served generous portions of spaghetti and meatballs to her family and Brian, who was staying for supper. She passed the bread and salad. For a while it was quiet. Everyone was busy eating.

"What're you going to name the baby?" Brian asked between forkfuls of spaghetti.

"I don't know," Danny answered.

"Baby! We're going to call it Baby!" said Missy.

"You can call it Baby, Missy, if you want to, but it has to have a better name than that," Danny's father said. "Your mother and I like Michael, if it's a boy, and Jennifer, if it's a girl. What do you think?"

"I bet it's a boy!" said Danny. "I bet on Michael."

"And I'm betting on Jennifer," Brian challenged him. "Wanna bet?"

"How much?"

"A candy bar."

"OK."

The boys shook hands and went back to enjoying their dinner.

When Danny got up to get a drink in the middle of the night, the lights were on in his parents' room. He heard his dad talking on the phone. "Hello, Mrs. Parks. . . . Yes, we're leaving for the hospital. Can you come right away? . . . Great!" Baby brother Michael would be arriving soon, Danny knew.

Only the newcomer was baby sister Jennifer instead. His dad said she had curly black hair like Danny's. "She's red-faced and tiny but really cute," he told Danny the next morning. "You'll love her."

Danny was not so sure.

"You win," he told Brian when he got to the bus stop. "It's Jennifer."

"Hey, great! You owe me a candy bar." Brian was pleased.

Danny sounded proud and happy, too, when he told the class about his baby sister during "What's on Your Mind?" Mrs. Abrams asked the students, "When a woman has a baby, what are the chances of its being a girl?"

"One out of two," answered a boy in the back.

"Not really," said Abigail. "More boys are born than girls—about one hundred and four boys to every hundred girls."

"I don't believe you," said Brian. "You made that up."

"No, I didn't. It says so in the encyclopedia."

"Yeah, I bet," Brian said. "I heard somewhere that when guys and girls are old enough to get married, there aren't enough guys to go around. How come, if there are more to begin with?"

"Easy," Abigail answered. "Girls are stronger and smarter and better in every way. They're tough. They last longer."

The girls clapped. The boys groaned. There were

more boys than girls in Mrs. Abrams' class. It took her a while to get the students started on the day's math lesson.

Danny had trouble concentrating. He couldn't wait to see his cute baby sister, maybe even hold her.

Brian nudged him. "You owe me a candy bar, remember? I want it with lunch."

"OK," Danny said. This was one time he didn't mind paying up.

Place Your Bets!

Here are ten situations that involve probability. What do you think will happen in each one? How good are you at figuring the chances and predicting the future? Turn to page 93 to find out whether you would have won or lost if you had bet.

1 ★ The next time Brian and Danny toss a coin, will Brian win the toss? Is tossing a coin a fair way for them to reach a decision?

2 ★ At this year's PTA carnival Brian bought five raffle tickets, but he did not win the TV set. Will his chances of winning the prize be better next year if he buys ten tickets? Since he'll be buying twice as many tickets, will his chances be twice as good?

3 ★ Seven isn't always lucky for Brian. Is seven a lucky number for anyone?

4 ★ One day Abigail shows Brian and Danny a spinner that looks like this. She says she will buy them a candy bar if the spinner stops on red, but if it stops on either blue or green they'll have to buy her two candy bars. Brian wants to play, but Danny says it isn't a fair game. Who is right?

5 ★ Brian says the odds against rolling any number from one to six with a single die are six to one. Is he right?

6 ★ The weather report for Saturday predicts a 40 percent chance of showers. Will the Little League play-off game be rained out?

7 ★ Last season Danny's batting average was .278. This year it is .270. Brian says it is .274 for the two years. Is he right?

8 ★ At the beginning of a rummy game Danny holds two threes, along with the seven and eight of clubs and other cards that don't match. Brian has the five and seven of diamonds and two jacks, along with other unmatched cards. Who is going to win this game?

9 ★ Danny is watching as Brian packs for two weeks at summer camp. He plans to take four pairs of shorts—blue cutoffs, black gym shorts, purple walkers, bright flowered "jams"—and six T-shirts, each with a different design. Danny says that gives Brian a total of ten possible outfits. Is Danny right?

10 ★ If Danny's mother has another baby, will it be a boy, to give Danny the brother he wants so much?

Your Chances: Are You a Winner?

1 ★ Each time one of the boys tosses a coin, the chance that it will land heads up is one out of two (1/2), the same as the chance that it will land tails up. Brian may win, or he may lose. Tossing a coin is a fair way to reach a decision because each boy has the same chance (1/2) of winning the toss.

2 ★ Brian's chances of winning are figured by dividing the number of tickets he bought by the total number of tickets sold. If exactly the same number of tickets is sold next year, his chances of winning will be twice as good if he buys twice as many. But that is not likely. If more than twice as many tickets are sold, Brian's chances will be even worse than they were this year. That is not very likely either. Buying more tickets will probably improve Brian's chances, but he still has to be lucky in order to win.

3 ★ Seven is no luckier than any other number. However, when a pair of dice is rolled, seven is more likely to turn up than any other number from two to twelve—one chance out of six (1/6) compared to one out of twelve (1/12) for a four or a ten, for example.

4 ★ Danny is right. Abigail's spinner game is not fair. Half the spinner is red. The other half is blue and green. The chances that the pointer will stop on red are two out of four or one out of two (2/4 = 1/2). The chances that it will stop in the blue and green area are

also two out of four or one out of two. Since the chances
for red are the same as for blue and green together, the
payoff should be the same too—one candy bar. A payoff of two candy bars would be fair if it stopped *only* on
blue, or *only* on green, because the chance that this will
happen is only one out of four (1/4), half the chance
that the pointer will stop on red.

5 ★ Brian is wrong. Odds are a way of expressing
probability, but odds are not expressed in the same way
as chances. With a single die there is one chance in six
that you will roll any given number from one to six.
That leaves five chances that you won't. The odds in
favor of rolling that number are one to five. The odds
against are five to one. When Brian and Danny were
tossing Danny's coin, there was one chance that the
coin would land heads up and one that it would land
tails up. The chances were one out of two, but the odds
were even—one in favor to one against, or one to one.

6 ★ The Little League game will probably be
played. With a 40 percent chance of showers, there is
still a 60 percent chance that it will not rain.

7 ★ Brian is wrong. To get the correct average, add the number of hits Danny made in the second season to the number of hits he made in the first. Then add the number of times he was at bat in the second season to the number of times at bat in the first. Divide the total number of hits by the total number of times at bat. The result would be Danny's batting average for the two years. You can't average batting averages.

8 ★ Danny seems to have the better hand because he can use one of two cards, either the six or the nine of clubs, to complete his sequence. Only one card, the six of diamonds, will complete Brian's. But it is only the beginning of the game. No one can tell who will win in the end.

9 ★ Danny is wrong. Each of the four pairs of shorts can be worn with *any* one of the six T-shirts. Multiply 4 by 6 to get 24, the total number of different

outfits Brian can make with the shorts and shirts he plans to take to camp. You can check this by listing all the combinations, using S1, S2, S3, S4 for the shorts and T1, T2, T3, T4, T5, T6 for the T-shirts. Of course, some of the outfits may look better than others!

10 ★ The chances are the same as before baby sister Jennifer was born—about one out of two. However, as Abigail pointed out in Mrs. Abrams' class, Danny has a slightly better chance of having a new baby brother. And other factors besides chance may influence the sex of a child.

Bibliography

Titles of special interest to young readers are marked with an asterisk (*).

*Brady, Maxine. *The Monopoly Book: Strategy and Tactics of the World's Most Popular Game*. New York: David McKay Co., Inc., 1974.

*Burns, Marilyn. *The I Hate Mathematics! Book*. Boston: Little, Brown and Company, 1975.

*———. *Math for Smarty Pants*. Boston: Little, Brown and Company, 1982.

*Garden, Nancy. *The Kids' Code and Cipher Book*. New York: Holt, Rinehart and Winston, 1981.

Levinson, Horace C. *Chance, Luck and Statistics*. New York: Dover Publications, 1963.

*Linn, Charles F. *Probability*. New York: Thomas Y. Crowell, 1972.

McGervey, John D. *Probabilities in Everyday Life*. Chicago: Nelson-Hall Publishers, 1986.

Neft, David S.; Richard M. Cohen; and Jordan A. Deutsch. *The World Book of Odds*. New York: Grosset & Dunlap, 1978.

Paulos, John Allen. *Innumeracy: Mathematical Illiteracy and Its Consequences*. New York: Hill & Wang, 1988.

*Razell, Arthur G., and K. G. O. Watts. *Probability: The Science of Chance*. Garden City, NY: Doubleday & Company, 1967.

*Reisberg, Ken. *Card Games*. New York: Franklin Watts, 1979.

*Riedel, Manfred G. *Odds and Chances for Kids: A Look at Probability*. Englewood Cliffs, NJ: Prentice-Hall, 1979.

*——. *Winning with Numbers: A Kid's Guide to Statistics*. Englewood Cliffs, NJ: Prentice-Hall, 1978.

Shulte, Albert P., and Stuart A. Choate. *What Are My Chances?* (Books A and B). Palo Alto, CA: Creative Publications, 1977.

*Srivastava, Jane Jonas. *Statistics*. New York: Thomas Y. Crowell, 1973.

Vergara, William C. *Mathematics in Everyday Things*. New York: Harper & Row, Publishers, 1959.

*Zim, Herbert S. *Codes and Secret Writing*. New York: William Morrow and Company, 1948.

Index